JACQUES DERRIDA

JACQUES DERRIDA

LEARNING TO LIVE FINALLY

THE LAST INTERVIEW

by JEAN BIRNBAUM
translated by PASCALE-ANNE BRAULT and MICHAEL NAAS
with a bibliography by PETER KRAPP

MELVILLE HOUSE
BROOKLYN, NEW YORK

LEARNING TO LIVE FINALLY

Originally published in French as *Apprendre à vivre enfin,
Entretien avec Jean Birnbaum* by Editions Galilée

© 2005 by Editions Galilée, Paris, France

Translation © 2007 by Pascale-Anne Brault and Michel Naas

First Melville House printing: May 2007

Melville House Publishing
145 Plymouth Street
Brooklyn, NY 11201

www.mhpbooks.com

ISBN: 978-1-61219-094-5

Printed in the United States of America

2 3 4 5 6 7 8 9 10

A catalog record for this book is available
from the Library of Congress

CONTENTS

INTRODUCTION
BEARING LOSS: DERRIDA AS A CHILD

BY JEAN BIRNBAUM

This is about a certain end. Let us then hasten to begin by the end.[1]

On August 19, 2004, the French newspaper *Le Monde* published an interview with Jacques Derrida. In that interview, which appeared under the title "I am at war with myself," the philosopher appeared on a scene that was familiar to him, that of a mourning at once originary and incessantly to come, and whose imminence now seemed to color his every gesture. On this scene or stage Derrida had chosen to come forward, this time more than ever, as a survivor. That is, as both an "uneducable specter who will have never learned how to live" and a man who does not want to stop saying "yes" to life, a thinker whose entire work pays homage to the subversive intensity of existence.

A few weeks after the publication of this interview, during the night of October 9, Derrida succumbed to his illness. For those who had read and loved him, and who were ready to accompany him further, for a long time still and always *in the present*, it wasn't easy to find the strength. At the moment the curtain fell, one felt, almost instinctively, that it was best not to move: better just to stay there by his side, on that inexorable stage of mourning where we would have to bid him "farewell [*salut*]."

Not to disappear from the scene, then, not to leave the stage. If I may thus be forgiven an apparent aside, I would like to recall here the name of Imre Kertesz and thank the theater company of the Théâtre Ouvert in Paris, where his *Kaddish for a Child Not Born* was adapted for the stage and performed.[2] As early as the end of August, the director of this national center for drama, Lucien Attoun, after having read the interview with Derrida in *Le Monde*, invited me to come hear the spectral writing of this Hungarian writer and recipient of the Nobel Prize for literature.[3] There was no coincidence in this generous invitation: in this *Kaddish* of Kertesz, in these wandering words of a man already half in the grave, what was inaugurated was indeed something like a *cogito of survival*: "I survived therefore I am." Everything is there if you listen carefully, everything returns in the form of some Derridean theme: "I was able to survive, or simply to be and exist, only in secret," confides the narrator of this strange *Kaddish*.

There would be much to say about these moments when the spectral writing of Kertesz seems inhabited, indeed literally ventriloquized, by the spirits (for there are more than one) of Derrida. Let me simply mark this double uncertainty, the double aporia with which the Hungarian author struggles: it is impossible, from childhood on, to know what it is "to be Jewish"—that's the original problem of identity; and it is also impossible to acquire, in the proper sense of the term, any kind of "*savoir-vivre*," any kind of "knowing how to live." No way *to learn to live* [*apprendre à vivre*], to take up the expression Kertesz uses repeatedly, never without italics, to describe the absolute solitude of his character, a former prisoner of the concentration camps, now a writer whose wife has left him: "She repeated more than once that it was from me that she *learned to live*," recalls the narrator of this *Kaddish* wherein the futility of such hope is expressed on every page.[4]

That's it for the end; now let's return to the beginning. A few months before this *coup de théâtre*, I went to the home of Jacques Derrida. It was the spring of 2004; the terrible illness was there but the hour of the Kaddish seemed far away. No one, at least, could really imagine it. After many hesitations, at the moment of beginning our conversation, of posing a first question, it was almost exactly the same words, the same italics, that imposed themselves upon us: "Someone, you or me, comes forward and says: *I would like to learn to live finally*."[5] Everything began there, everything being contained there in reserve, in this enigmatic formula that gave the interview its initial impetus and its momentum.

That the philosopher himself wished to confer upon his responses a sort of testamentary charge was clear from the outset. To rediscover them today, in light of the Kaddish, is to confront the affirmation and hope that are displayed there, no matter the cost, one line after another: the lucid affirmation of a death that is coming, always already there, impossible to anticipate; hope in an unrelenting fidelity—an entrusted trace, a renewed promise. It is here that we find again the theme of transmission, of legacy, the "politics of memory, of inheritance, and of generations" that is sought in Derrida's *Specters of Marx*, on the horizon of an obligation to justice and an endless responsibility before "the ghosts of those who are not yet born or who are already dead."[6]

This archive desire, this essential concern for generations, haunts the entire Derridean landscape. From out of this landscape two figures emerge, those of the ghost and of the child—the only witnesses at the end. To follow the traces they leave behind, let us return briefly to the two aporias of Imre Kertesz's *Kaddish*.

First, Jewishness: a "lost child" of Judaism, Derrida often recalled the double movement of acquiescence and anxiety, of love and revolt, that characterized his relationship to the tradition of Israel. Evoking in this regard "the obscure and uncertain experience of inheritance," he underscored the violence of an assignation of identity inscribed from the outset in the immemorial time of an interminable repetition, and first of all in "the memory without memory of circumcision." A so very dangerous assignation that seizes, "harpoons," and threatens (with death) the Jewish child "before any fault and before any act," that is, we might say, before even any *act of birth*.[7] Called thus into a covenant, as if prior to any coming into the world, all those who bear a Jewish name find themselves in what Derrida calls "the situation of an at once spectral and patriarchic nursling."[8]

And then: *learning to live*. As with Jewishness, we would have to cite text after text on this point, so much is Derrida's reflection obsessed by this second aporia, this other way of naming the impossible: "To live, by definition, is not something one learns. Not from oneself, it is not learned from life, taught by life. Only from the other and by death."[9] Living, like dying, is not something one learns. All one can really do is see it coming. Together. To try to *learn from one another* to live, in a shared anxiety and a difficult freedom, where each *expects him or herself* to die: a passing out of life, farewell [*salut*] in the night. Whence the renewed necessity not to distinguish between these two silhouettes: the specter and the child. Not only, of course, because whoever goes through the trial of death prepares to take the *step beyond*—"as disarmed as a newly born child"—but also and especially because the task of every survivor, that is, of the one who temporarily survives the other, the friend, consists in enduring his or her disappearance.[10] This survivor prepares to bear (*tragen*) the absence—or, better, *to bear the loss as one bears a child*.[11]

Such is the burning vocation of the survivor, this apprentice ghost who never looks backward without falling back into childhood: "survival structures every instant in a kind of irreducible torsion, that of a retrospective anticipation that introduces the untimely moment and the posthumous into what is most living in the living present, the rearview mirror of an expecting-death at every moment," writes Derrida.[12]

A few days before the publication of our interview (which here appears in its entirety and as Derrida himself had approved it), the philosopher was seated at a table at his home in Ris-Orangis. Pen in hand, he reread the contents of the interview with great care, with the studious concentration of someone who always wanted to present himself as a schoolboy. Wherever a particular formulation had been edited out, we would be certain to be reproached: "Do you realize the vertiginous questions contained in these words?"

His eyes were full of a gentle anger, simple, almost innocent. And he would try to catch the eye, to gain the support, of his wife, Marguerite, without whom nothing would have been possible.

In this text, Derrida had wanted to speak of his illness. Did he sense that it would be for both the first and last time? One might think so, given how painful each deletion was to him. Time was running out on all sides: he was expected that afternoon in Brazil, where an international conference was being held in his honor. His suitcases still open, he took a moment to sit down and heave a sigh: "One thing is certain, people are going to read this and think I'm just barely surviving, that I am already dead." We took these words at the time as a sort of provocation from an *enfant terrible*. No one close to him could really believe it.

A week later, upon his return from Rio de Janeiro, he was given the interview as it had just appeared in *Le Monde*. Several times he confided to those close to him that he was at once pleased and disheartened: "It's an obituary," he sighed, using this blunt assessment to counter the objections of his friends: "No,

Jacques," they argued, "it's only a trace, and it's a trace of life." And in fact, if you listen again today to the tapes on which our interview was recorded, it is indeed the voice of Derrida you hear, perfectly intact, the same as it always was. The voice of a *ghost* that is already contemplating the irreparable. Cheerful and gentle, it is the voice of a *spectral child* who does not yet know anything about life, and who is just beginning to learn—finally: "I see myself dead cut off from you in your memories that I love and I weep like my own children at the edge of my grave..."[13]

JEAN BIRNBAUM

LEARNING TO LIVE FINALLY

JEAN BIRNBAUM: Since summer 2003 you've never been more visible on the public scene. You have not only published many new works but have traveled around the world to participate in several international conferences organized around your work—in London, in Coimbra, here in Paris, and, in the coming days, in Rio de Janeiro. A second film has been made about you (*Derrida* by Amy Kofman and Kirby Dirk, after Safaa Fathy's very beautiful 2000 film, *Derrida's Elsewhere*), and several publications have devoted special issues to your work, including *Le magazine littéraire*, the journal *Europe*, and a volume of the *Cahiers de l'Herne*, which contains a number of unpublished works. That's quite a lot for a single year, and yet you haven't hidden the fact that you are . . .

JACQUES DERRIDA: . . . you can just say it, very seriously ill, and undergoing a very aggressive treatment. But let's leave that aside, if you don't mind, we are not here to issue a medical report—whether public or secret . . .

JB: Fine. Here at the outset of our interview, then, let's return instead to *Specters of Marx*. A crucial book, a defining work devoted entirely to the question of a justice to come, and which begins with this enigmatic exordium: "Someone, you or me, comes forward and says: *I would like to learn to live finally*." More than ten years later, where are you today with regard to this desire to "know how to live"?

JD: At the time—this was in 1993—what was at issue was a "new international," the subtitle and a central theme of the book. Beyond "cosmopolitanism," beyond the notion of a "world citizen," beyond a new world nation-state, even beyond the logic, in the final analysis, of political "parties," this book anticipates

all the "alter-globalist" imperatives in which I believe
and which appear more clearly today (though still in-
sufficiently, in a chaotic and unthought way).[14] What
I called at that time a "new international" would re-
quire, I argued back in 1993, a large number of muta-
tions in international law and in all the organizations
that establish world order (IMF, WTO, the G8, and
especially the United Nations and its Security Coun-
cil, whose charter would have to be changed for start-
ers, along with its autonomous forces of intervention,
its composition, and first of all its location—as far
away as possible from New York City...)

As for the phrase you just cited ("learning to live
finally [*apprendre à vivre enfin*]"), it came to me once
the book was finished. It plays first of all, though in
a serious way, on its everyday meaning. *Apprendre à
vivre* means to mature, but also to educate: to teach
someone else and especially oneself. When you address someone and say "*je vais t'apprendre à vivre*," it
sometimes has a threatening tone, meaning not only
"I am going to teach you how to live" but "I'm going to teach you a lesson," "I'm going to get you to
shape up or whip you into shape." From there—and
the ambiguity of this play is even more important

to me—this sigh leads to a more difficult question: is living something that can be *learned*? or *taught*? Can one learn, through discipline or apprenticeship, through experience or experimentation, to *accept* or, better, to *affirm* life? This concern for legacy and death resonates throughout the entire book. It is also something that torments parents and their children: "When will you become responsible? How will you *answer* or finally *take responsibility* for your life and for your name?"

So, to finally answer your question, no, I never *learned-to-live*. In fact not at all! Learning to live should mean learning to die, learning to take into account, so as to accept, absolute mortality (that is, without salvation, resurrection, or redemption—neither for oneself nor for the other). That's been the old philosophical injunction since Plato: to philosophize is to learn to die. I believe in this truth without being able to resign myself to it. And less and less so. I have never learned to accept it, to accept death, that is. We are all survivors who have been granted a temporary reprieve [*en sursis*] (and, from the geopolitical perspective of *Specters of Marx*, this is especially true, in a world that is more inegalitarian than ever, for the millions and millions of living beings—human or not—who are denied not only their basic "human rights," which date back two centuries and are constantly being refined, but first of all the right to a life worthy of being lived). But I remain uneducable when it comes to any kind of wisdom about knowing-how-to-die or, if you prefer, knowing-how-to-live. I still have not learned or picked up anything on this subject. The time of the reprieve is rapidly running out. Not just because I am, along with others, the heir of so many things, some good, some quite terrible: but since most of the thinkers with whom I have been associated are now dead, I am referred to more and more often as a *survivor*—the last, the final representative of a "generation," that is, roughly speaking, the sixties generation. Without being strictly speaking true, this provokes in me not only objections but feelings of a somewhat melancholic revolt. In addition, since certain health problems have become, as we were saying, so urgent, the question of survival [*la survie*] or of reprieve [*le sursis*], a question that has always haunted me, literally *every instant* of my life, in a concrete and unrelenting fashion, has come to have a different resonance today. I have always been

interested in this theme of survival, the meaning of
which is *not to be added on* to living and dying. It is
originary: life *is* living on, life *is* survival [la vie *est* sur-
vie]. To survive in the usual sense of the term means
to continue to live, but also to live *after* death. When
it comes to translating such a notion, Benjamin em-
phasizes the distinction between *überleben*, on the
one hand, surviving death, like a book that survives
the death of its author, or a child the death of his or
her parents, and, on the other hand, *fortleben, living on*, continuing to live. All the concepts that have
helped me in my work, and notably that of the trace
or of the spectral, were related to this "surviving" as
a structural and rigorously originary dimension. It is
not derived from either living or dying. No more than
what I call "originary mourning," that is, a mourning
that does not wait for the so-called "actual" death.

JB: You used the word "generation." It's a rather tricky
notion that comes up quite often in your writing:
how is one to refer to what is, in your name, passed
on from a generation?

JD: It's a word I use here rather loosely. One can be

the "anachronistic" contemporary of a past or future "generation." To be faithful to those associated with my "generation," to be the guardian of a differentiated and yet common heritage, can mean two things: first, to adhere, sometimes in opposition to everyone and everything, to certain shared exigencies, from Lacan to Althusser, and including Levinas, Foucault, Barthes, Deleuze, Blanchot, Lyotard, Sarah Kofman, and so on, not to mention all those writer-thinkers, poets, philosophers, or psychoanalysts, fortunately still living, from whom I also inherit, both in France— all those, for example, who contributed to the works you had the kindness to mention in the beginning (we must ask them to forgive us for not being able to say more about them here)—and then abroad, more numerous and sometimes closer (I could cite dozens of names here, often more important for me than many French). I am referring here, by metonymy, to an *ethos* of writing and of thinking, an intransigent or indeed incorruptible *ethos* (Hélène Cixous calls us the "incorruptibles"), without any concession even to philosophy, an *ethos* that does not let itself be scared off by what public opinion, the media, or the phantasm of an intimidating readership might pressure one to

NB

simplify or repress. Whence the strict taste for refine-
ment, paradox, and aporia. This predilection also remains an obligation. It unites not only those I just
mentioned a bit arbitrarily, which is to say, unjustly,
but the entire milieu that supported them. We are
talking about a sort of *provisionally bygone era*, and
not about such and such a person. It is thus necessary
to save that or bring it back to life, at any cost. And
the responsibility for this is today so urgent: it calls
for an unrelenting war against *doxa*, against those
who are today called "media intellectuals," against a
general discourse that has been preformatted by media powers that are themselves in the hands of certain
politico-economic, editorial, and academic lobbies.
At once European and global. Resistance does not
mean that one ought to avoid the media. One must,
whenever possible, develop them and help them to
diversify, to recall them to this same responsibility.

At the same time, we must not forget that that
"happy" era of yesteryear was hardly a time of peace
and tranquility. Indeed far from it. Differences and
differends ran rampant in that milieu, which was
anything but a homogeneous whole that might be
summed up by some idiotic term like "1968 thought,"

a term that today dominates both the press and the university as either a rallying cry or an indictment. So, even if this fidelity still sometimes takes the form of infidelity and a parting of ways, one must be faithful to these differences, that is, one must keep the discussion going. As for me, I continue to discuss, for example, Bourdieu, Lacan, Deleuze, and Foucault, whom I continue to find much more interesting than those with whom the press is so impressed today (there are, of course, exceptions). I am keeping this debate alive, trying to prevent it from becoming stale or degenerating into simple deprecation.

What I say about my generation holds just as well, of course, for the past, from the Bible to Plato, Kant, Marx, Freud, Heidegger, and so on. I don't want to renounce anything, indeed I cannot. Because, you know, learning to live is always *narcissistic* (a concept, let me just note in passing, that I've tried to complicate elsewhere): one wants to live as much as possible, to save oneself, to persevere, and to cultivate all these things which, though infinitely greater and more powerful than oneself, nonetheless form a part of this little "me" that they exceed on all sides. To ask me to renounce what formed me, what I've loved so much,

what has been my law, is to ask me to die. In this
fidelity there is a sort of instinct for self-preservation.
To renounce, for example, some difficult formulation,
some complication, paradox, or supplementary contradiction, because it is not going to be understood,
or rather because some journalist who does not know
how to read it, or read even the title of a book, thinks
he or she understands that the reader or audience will
not understand any better, and that his or her ratings
and job will suffer as a result, is for me an unacceptable obscenity. It is as if I were being asked to capitu-
late or to subjugate myself—or else to die of stupidity.

JB: You have invented a form of writing, a writing
of survival [*survivance*], which is suited to this impa-
tience of fidelity. A writing of the inherited promise,
of the safeguarded trace, and of entrusted responsibility.

JD: If I had invented my writing, I would have done
so as a perpetual revolution. For it is necessary in
each situation to create an appropriate mode of expo-
sition, to invent the law of the singular event, to take
into account the presumed or desired addressee; and,

at the same time, to make as if this writing will de-
termine the reader, who will learn to read (to "live")
something he or she was not accustomed to receiving
from anywhere else. One hopes that he or she will be
reborn differently, determined otherwise, as a result:
for example, these grafts of poetry onto philosophy,
which are anything but confused, or certain ways of
using homonyms, the undecidable, or the ruses of
language, which many read in confusion because they
fail to recognize their properly *logical necessity*. Each
book is a pedagogy aimed at forming its reader. The
mass productions that today inundate the press and
publishing houses do not form their readers; they pre-
suppose in a phantasmatic and rudimentary fashion a
reader who has already been programmed. They thus
end up preformatting this very mediocre addressee
whom they had postulated in advance.

And yet, out of a concern for fidelity, as you say,
at the moment of leaving a trace I cannot but make
it available to whomever: I cannot even address it *in
a singular fashion* to someone. Each time, however
faithful one might want to be, one ends up betraying
the singularity of the other whom one is addressing.
The same goes *a fortiori* when one writes books for a

more general audience: you do not know to whom you are speaking, you invent and create silhouettes, but in the end it no longer belongs to you. Spoken or written, all these gestures leave us and begin to act independently of us. Like machines or, better, like marionettes (I try to explain this in *Paper Machine*). At the moment I leave "my" book (to be published)—after all, no one forces me to do it—I become, appearing-disappearing, like that uneducable specter who will have never learned how to live. The trace I leave signifies to me at once my death, either to come or already come upon me, and the hope that this trace survives me. This is not a striving for immortality; it's something structural. I leave a piece of paper behind, I go away, I die: it is impossible to escape this structure, it is the unchanging form of my life. Each time I let something go, each time some trace leaves me, "proceeds" from me, unable to be reappropriated, I live my death in writing. It's the ultimate test: one expropriates oneself without knowing exactly who is being entrusted with what is left behind. Who is going to inherit, and how? Will there even be any heirs?

This question is more relevant today than ever before. It preoccupies me constantly. But the time of our techno-culture has radically changed in this regard. The people of my "generation," and *a fortiori* those of previous ones, had been accustomed to a certain historical rhythm: one thought one knew that a particular work might or might not survive, based upon its own qualities, for one, two, or, perhaps, like Plato, twenty-five centuries. Disappear, then be reborn. But today, the acceleration in the forms of archivization, though also use and destruction, are transforming the structure, temporality, and duration of the legacy. When it comes to thought, the question of survival has taken on absolutely unforeseeable forms. At my age, I am ready to entertain the most contradictory hypotheses in this regard: I have simultaneously—I ask you to believe me on this—the *double feeling* that, on the one hand, to put it playfully and with a certain immodesty, one has not yet begun to read me, that even though there are, to be sure, many very good readers (a few dozen in the world perhaps, people who are also writer-thinkers, poets), in the end it is later on that all this has a chance of appearing; but also, on the other hand, and thus simultaneously, I have the feeling that two weeks or a month after my death *there will be nothing left*. Nothing except what has been copyrighted and deposited in libraries. I swear to you, I believe sincerely and simultaneously in these two hypotheses.

JB: At the heart of this hope there is language, and first of all the French language. When reading you, one can feel in every line the intensity of your passion for this language. In *Monolinguism of the Other* you go so far as to call yourself, with a certain irony, the "last defender and illustrator of the French language."[15]

JD: Which does not belong to me, even though it's the only one I "have" at my disposal (and even then!). The experience of language is, of course, vital. And thus mortal. Nothing original in that. A series of contingencies have made of me a French Jew from Algeria born in the generation before the "war of independence": so many singularities, even among Jews, and even among the Jews of Algeria. I was part of an extraordinary transformation of French Judaism in Algeria: my great grandparents were still very close to the Arabs in language and customs. At the end of the nineteenth century, in the years following the

Crémieux decree of 1870, the next generation became more bourgeois: though my grandmother had to be married more or less clandestinely in the back court-yard of a town hall in Algiers because of the pogroms (this was right in the middle of the Dreyfus affair), she was already raising her daughters like bourgeois Parisian girls (16ᵗʰ Arrondissement good manners, piano lessons, and so on). Then came my parents' generation: few intellectuals, mostly shopkeepers, some of modest means and some not, and some who were already exploiting a colonial situation by becoming the exclusive representatives of major metropolitan brands: with a tiny little office and no secretary, one could, for example, become the sole distributor of all the "Marseille soap" in Northern Africa (I'm of course simplifying a bit). Then came my generation (a majority of intellectuals: liberal professions, teaching, medicine, law, etc.). And in 1962 just about everyone in France.[16] I myself had come earlier, in 1949. It was with me—I'm hardly exaggerating—that "mixed" marriages began. In a quasi-tragic, revolutionary, rare, and risky fashion. And just as I love life, and my life, I love what made me what I am, the very element of which is language, this French language that is the only language I was ever taught to cultivate, the only one also for which I can say I am more or less responsible. That is why there is in my writing a certain, I wouldn't say perverse but somewhat violent, way of treating this language. Out of love. Love in general passes by way of the love of language, which is neither nationalistic nor conservative, but which demands testimonials—and trials. You don't just go and do anything with language; it preexists us and it survives us. When you introduce something into language, you have to do it in a refined manner, by respecting through disrespect its secret law. That's what might be called unfaithful fidelity: when I do violence to the French language, I do so with the refined respect of what I believe to be an injunction of this language, in its life and in its evolution. I always have to laugh, though sometimes with contempt, when I read those who think they are violating, precisely without love, the "classic" spelling or syntax of a certain French language; they always look a little like virgin boys given to premature ejaculation, while the great French language, more untouchable than ever, watches on and awaits the next in line. I describe this ridiculous scene in a rather cruel way in *The Post Card*.[17]

To leave traces in the history of the French language—that's what interests me. I live off this passion, that is, if not for France at least for something that the French language has incorporated for centuries. I think that if I love this language like I love my life, and sometimes more than certain native French do, it is because I love it as a foreigner who has been welcomed, and who has appropriated this language for himself as the only possible language for him. Passion and hyperbolization. All the French of Algeria share this with me, whether Jewish or not: those who came from metropolitan France were nonetheless foreigners—oppressors and standardizers, normalizers and moralizers. They provided a model, a uniform and a uniformity, a *habitus*, and one had to conform to it. But at the same time we made fun of the French from France. When a teacher arrived from the *Métropole* with his French accent we found him ridiculous![18] That's where the hyperbolization comes in: I have only one language, and, at the same time, in an at once singular and exemplary fashion, this language does not belong to me. I explain this better in *Monolinguism of the Other*. A singular history has exacerbated in me this universal law: a language is not something that belongs. Not naturally and in its essence. Whence the phantasms of property, appropriation, and colonialist imposition.

JB: In general, you seem to have a hard time saying "we"—for example, "we philosophers" or "we Jews." But as the new world disorder unfolds, you seem less and less reticent to say "we Europeans." Already in *The Other Heading*, a book written during the first Gulf War, you spoke of yourself as an "old European," as "a sort of European hybrid."[19]

JD: Two reminders: I do indeed have a hard time saying "we," but there are occasions when I do say it. In spite of all the problems that torment me on this subject, beginning with the disastrous and suicidal politics of Israel and of a certain Zionism (for there have been more than one, since the very beginning, and Israel does not represent to my eyes Judaism as a whole any more than it represents the world diaspora, or even world Zionism or an originary Zionism, which was multiple and contradictory; there are in fact fundamentalist Christians in the United States who claim to be authentic Zionists, and the power of their lobby matters more to the Bush administration than the American Jewish community, not to mention the Saudis, when it comes to determining the joint direction of American-Israeli politics), well, in spite of all that and so many other problems I have with my "Jewishness," I will *never* deny it. I will always say, in certain situations, "we Jews." This so very tormented "we" is at the heart of what is most worried in my thought, the thought of someone I once called, with just a bit of a smile, "the last of the Jews." It would be, in my thought, like what Aristotle says so profoundly of prayer [*eukhe*]: it is neither true nor false. It is, in fact, literally a prayer. In certain situations, then, I do not hesitate to say "we Jews," as well as "we French."

Then also, since the very beginning of my work—and this would be "deconstruction" itself—I have remained extremely critical with regard to Europeanism or Eurocentrism, especially in certain modern formulations of it, for example, in Valéry, Husserl, or Heidegger. I have written a great deal on this subject and in this direction (especially in *The Other Heading*). Deconstruction in general is an undertaking that many have considered, and rightly so, to be a

gesture of suspicion with regard to all Eurocentrism.
When more recently I have had occasion to say "we
Europeans" it is something quite different and is
always related to a particular set of circumstances:
everything that can be deconstructed in the European tradition does not negate the possibility—and
precisely because of what has happened in Europe,
because of the Enlightenment, because of the shrink-
ing of this little continent and the enormous guilt
that pervades its culture (totalitarianism, Nazism, fas-
cism, genocides, Shoah, colonization and decoloniza-
tion, etc.)—that today, in the geopolitical situation
in which we find ourselves, Europe, an other Europe
but with the same memory, might (this is in any case
my wish) band together against both the politics of
American hegemony (in the configuration Wolfowitz,
Cheney, Rumsfield, and so on) and an Arab-Islamic
theocratism without Enlightenment and without political future (though let's not minimize the contra-
dictions, the processes underway, and the heteroge-
neities within these two groups, and let us join forces
with those who resist from within these two blocs).

Europe finds itself under the injunction to assume a new responsibility. I am not speaking of the

European Community as it now exists or is taking shape in its current (neoliberal) majority, virtually threatened by so many internal wars (I remain very pessimistic in this regard), but of a Europe to come, a Europe trying to find itself. In ("geographical") Europe and elsewhere. What we call in a certain algebraic shorthand "Europe" has certain responsibilities to assume, for the future of humanity and the future of international law—that's my faith, my belief. In this case, I do not hesitate to say "we Europeans." It's not a question of hoping for the creation of a Europe that would be another military superpower, protecting its market and acting as a counterweight to other blocs, but of a Europe that would be able to sow the seeds of a new alter-globalist politics. Which is for me the only possible way out.

This force is underway. Even if its motivations are still confused, I don't think anything can now stop it. That's what I mean when I say Europe: an alter-globalist Europe, transforming the concept and practices of sovereignty and international law. And having at its disposal a genuine armed force, independent of NATO and of the United States, a military power that is neither offensive nor defensive nor even preventive and that would be able to intervene without delay in support of a new United Nations whose resolutions are finally respected (for example, for this is most urgent, in Israel, though elsewhere as well). This is also the place from which we might best think certain forms of secularism [*laïcité*], for example, or social justice, so many European legacies.

(I just mentioned "secularism." Please allow me a long parenthesis here. It is not about the veil at school but about the veil of "marriage." I unhesitatingly supported and endorsed with my signature the welcome and courageous initiative taken by Noël Mamère, even though same-sex marriage is an example of that great tradition inaugurated by Americans in the nineteenth century under the name of *civil disobedience*: not defiance of the Law but disobedience with regard to some legislative provision in the name of a better or higher law—whether to come or already written into the spirit or letter of the Constitution.[20] And so I "signed" in this current legislative context because it seems to me unjust for the rights of homosexuals, as well as hypocritical and ambiguous in both letter and spirit. If I were a legislator, I would propose simply getting rid of the word and concept of "marriage" in our civil and secular code. "Marriage" as a religious, sacred, heterosexual value—with a vow to procreate, to be eternally faithful, and so on—is a concession made by the secular state to the Christian church, and particularly with regard to monogamy, which is neither Jewish (it was imposed upon Jews by Europeans only in the nineteenth century and was not an obligation just a few generations ago in Jewish Maghreb), nor, as is well known, Muslim. By getting rid of the word and concept of "marriage," and thus this ambiguity or this hypocrisy with regard to the religious and the sacred—things that have no place in a secular constitution—one could put in their place a contractual "civil union," a sort of generalized *pacs*, one that has been improved, refined, and would remain flexible and adaptable to partners whose sex and number would not be prescribed.[21] As for those who want to be joined in "marriage" in the strict sense of the term—something, by the way, for which my respect remains totally intact—they would be able to do so before the religious authority of their choosing. This is already the case in certain countries where religiously consecrated same-sex marriages are allowed. Some people might thus unite according to one mode or the other, some according to both, others according to neither secular law nor religious law. So much for my little conjugal paragraph. It's utopic, but I'm already setting a date!)

What I call "deconstruction," even when it is directed toward something from Europe, is European; it is a product of Europe, a relation of Europe to itself as an experience of radical alterity. Since the time of the Enlightenment, Europe has undertaken a perpetual self-critique, and in this perfectible heritage there is a chance for a future. At least I would like to hope so, and that is what feeds my indignation when I hear people definitively condemning Europe as if it were but the scene of its crimes.

JB: With regard to Europe, are you not at war with yourself? On the one hand, you note that the attacks of September 11th are destroying the old geopolitical grammar of sovereign powers, thereby signaling the crisis of a certain concept of the political, which you define as properly European. On the other hand, you remain attached to this European spirit, and first of all to the cosmopolitical ideal of an international law whose decline you describe, or whose survival . . .

JD: The cosmopolitical has to be "raised to a new level" (*aufheben*) (see, for example, "On Cosmopolitanism").[22] When we speak of the political we are using a Greek word, a European concept that has always presupposed the state, the form of a *polis* linked to a national territory and to autochthony. Whatever ruptures there may be within this history, this concept of the political remains dominant even at the very moment so many forces are in the process of dismantling it: the sovereignty of the state is no longer linked to a territory, nor are today's communication technologies or military strategy, and this dislocation does in fact bring about a crisis in the old European concept of the political. And the same can be said for the concept of war, or the distinction between civilian and military, or national or international terrorism. I try to explain this at some length elsewhere (for example, in *Rogues* and in the interview I gave after 9-11).[23] But I don't think we should just take it out on the political. And I would say the same for sovereignty, which I believe in some situations can be a good thing, for example, in fighting against certain global market forces. Here again we are talking about a European legacy that must be at once retained and transformed.

I argue something similar in *Rogues* with regard to democracy as a European idea, something that at once has never existed in a satisfactory way and remains to come. And, in fact, you will always find this gesture in my work, and I have no ultimate justification for it, except to say that it's me, that that's where I am. I am at war with myself, it's true, you couldn't possibly know to what extent, beyond what you can guess, and I say contradictory things that are, we might say, in real tension; they are what construct me, make me live, and will make me die. I sometimes see this war as terrifying and difficult to bear, but at the same time I know that that is life. I will find peace only in eternal rest. I thus cannot really say that I assume this contradiction, but I know that it is what keeps me alive, and makes me ask precisely the question you recalled earlier, "how does one learn to live?"

JB: There is in your work a very old reflection on the relationship between knowledge and power, between research institutions and the state. Here again it seems to be from a certain European promise that your faith in "the Humanities of tomorrow" ("The University Without Condition") is renewed.[24]

JD: What I call the university of tomorrow, which must not be a conservatory, presupposes that teaching take on the mission inscribed in its very concept. A European and relatively modern concept that ordered the university to organize its search for truth without any conditions attached. That is, to be free to know, criticize, ask questions, and doubt without being limited by any political or religious power. The defining moment can be found in Kant, who puts philosophy in the lowest class, below medicine, law, and, of course, theology, because it is the furthest removed from power, but who grants it a certain superiority insofar as it must be free to say everything it considers to be true, on the condition that it says it within the university and not outside it—and that was my objection to Kant. In the originary concept of the university there is this absolute claim to an unconditional freedom to think, speak, and critique.

JB: But then what are we to do in the case of Holocaust revisionists who deny the existence of gas chambers and the reality of the Shoah?

JD: One has the right to ask all questions. But when

one responds to questions with falsifications or coun-
ter-truths, gestures that have nothing to do with hon-
est research or critical thought, then that's something
else. It's either incompetence or unjustified instru-
mentalism, and it has to be reprimanded, just as a bad
student has to be reprimanded. It's not because one
has the status of professor that one can say whatever
one wants in the university, even though we must
reserve for the university the possibility of posing
questions and reexamining things. If Faurisson had
simply said: "Let me have the right to do historical
research, let me have the right not to take certain witnesses at their word," then I would have been all for
letting him work.[25] But when he then wants, against a
mountain of evidence, to go from these critical questions to affirmations that are unacceptable from the
point of view of attested and proven truth, then he is
simply incompetent, harmful as well, but first of all
incompetent. And thus unworthy of presenting himself as a university professor. In this case, debate is impossible. But, in principle, the university remains the
only place where critical debate must remain uncon-
ditionally open. This is a legacy I hold dear, even if my
own relation to the university is rather complicated.

It is a legacy from Europe and from Greek philosophy; it was not born elsewhere. And despite all the deconstructive questions I pose with regard to this philosophy, I continue to say a certain yes to it, and I will never propose simply jettisoning it. I have never turned my back on either philosophy or Europe. My gestures are of another sort. I will never say—and you know what I'm referring to here—"Forget Europe! Goodbye [*salut*], philosophy!". . . No more than I will ever say "marriage is a fundamental value for society."

JB: In two recent works (*Chaque fois unique, la fin du monde* and "Rams"), you return to this important question of *salut* [farewell, greeting, salvation], of impossible mourning, in short, of survival.[26] If philosophy can be defined as the "attentive anticipation of death" (see *The Gift of Death*), might not deconstruction be considered an interminable ethics of the survivor? [27]

JD: *The Gift of Death* was meant to be, among many other things (for example, a new critical reinterpretation of responsibility as, according to Patocka, something essentially Europeo-Christian), an attempt to give another reading of Kierkegaard's Abraham. Despite my enormous admiration for this thinker, I tried to show that he perhaps Christianized the story of the binding of Isaac. I regret not having treated there and then the question of Christian marriage, as I have recently done in *Le Parjure* (just published in the *Cahier de l'Herne*).

As I recalled earlier, already from the beginning, and well before the experiences of surviving [*survivance*] that are at the moment mine, I maintained that survival is an originary concept that constitutes the very structure of what we call existence, *Dasein*, if you will. We are structurally survivors, marked by this structure of the trace and of the testament. But, having said that, I would not want to encourage an interpretation that situates surviving on the side of death and the past rather than life and the future. No, deconstruction is always on the side of the *yes*, on the side of the affirmation of life. Everything I say—at least from "*Pas*" (in *Parages*) on—about survival as a complication of the opposition life/death proceeds in me from an unconditional affirmation of life.[28] This surviving is life beyond life, life more than life, and my discourse is not a discourse of death, but, on the contrary, the affirmation of a living being who prefers living and thus surviving to death, because survival is not simply that which remains but the most intense life possible. I am never more haunted by the necessity of dying than in moments of happiness and joy. To feel joy and to weep over the death that awaits are for me the same thing. When I recall my life, I tend to think that I have had the good fortune to love even the unhappy moments of my life, and to bless them. Almost all of them, with just one exception. When I recall the happy moments, I bless them too, of course, at the same time as they propel me toward the thought of death, toward death, because all that has passed, come to an end ...

TRANSLATORS' NOTE

"I leave a piece of paper behind, I go away, I die: it is impossible to escape this structure, it is the unchanging form of my life. Each time I let something go, each time some trace leaves me, 'proceeds' from me, unable to be reappropriated, I live my death in writing." So said Jacques Derrida in the course of an interview with Jean Birnbaum of *Le Monde* during the summer of 2004. Expressed here in a particularly pointed and personal form is a claim about the nature of writing—indeed about the trace more generally—that can be found already in some of Derrida's earliest works. In his 1971 essay "Signature Event Context," for example, Derrida argued that writing "must continue to 'act' and to be readable even if what is called the author of the writing no longer answers for what he has written, for what he seems to have signed, whether he is provisionally absent, or if he is dead."[29] Though Derrida always insisted that this readability of the trace in the absence of the author is "structural" and not contingent upon the actual death of the author, that the author's disappearance or death is implied in the trace whether he or she is already dead *or* still living, this final iteration of the claim during the summer of 2004 holds for us today an exemplary, even a testamentary value. Published here in English for the first time under the title *Learning to Live Finally*, Derrida's interview with *Le Monde* both bears witness to his claim about the repeatability and survival of the trace and puts it to the test of a unique and unrepeatable event. For if Derrida's death in October of 2004 changed nothing about the status of the trace or of his own writing, it will have changed much about how we are to receive, read, and translate him today.

This is the place where, in several previous works over the past two decades, we took the opportunity to thank Jacques Derrida *personally* for the encouragement and help he gave us in the translation of his work, help understanding his original French and, oftentimes, help finding an appropriate English translation. This time—this time for the first time— we could benefit from no such help, not from the author of the work and not from the one we always considered to be our first reader. While we will thus continue to feel and to express our gratitude for the life and work of Jacques Derrida, and while we will continue to look to his other works for clues about how to read and translate him, we must now rely more than ever on the help and readings of others.

We would thus like to thank our students at De-Paul University for the many fine suggestions they made on the translation, both in a graduate seminar in philosophy at DePaul and during a Study Abroad program in Paris. Martin Hägglund of Cornell University also gave us many helpful comments on an earlier draft of the translation, as did Jean Birnbaum, who was able to supplement the written word with recollections of his spoken interview with Derrida.

Finally, we would like to offer our heartfelt thanks to Marguerite Derrida, who knows better than anyone what Jacques Derrida meant in his final interview when he spoke not only of a certain *hope* for the survival of his work but of an essential and irreducible *uncertainty* regarding its ultimate destiny and destination: for whenever one writes, said Derrida in August of 2004, "one expropriates oneself without knowing exactly who is being entrusted with what is left behind. Who is going to inherit, and how? Will there even be any heirs?"

PASCALE-ANNE BRAULT AND MICHAEL NAAS

NOTES

1   [Birnbaum's French title is "*Porter le deuil*," an idiom meaning
    to be in mourning or *to go into mourning*. Birnbaum, following
    Derrida, is playing on the fact that "*porter*" by itself means to
    carry or bear and can be used to describe the carrying or bear-
    ing of a child.—TR.]

2   Let me recall that, in the Jewish tradition, the Kaddish is a
    prayer of sanctification recited in particular during the period
    of mourning. *Kaddish for a Child Not Born*, trans. Christopher
    C. Wilson and Katharina M. Wilson (Evanston, IL: Hydra
    Books, 1997).
        The play performed at the Théâtre Ouvert was directed by
    Joël Jounneau, who, with Jean Launay, was also responsible for
    the script. The actor was Jean-Quentin Châtelain.

3   [Kertesz was awarded the Nobel Prize in Literature in 2002.
    —TR.]

4   [Or "That it was I who *taught* her how to live." As Derrida
    points out at the beginning of the interview, "*apprendre*" can
    mean either to *learn* or to *teach*, so that "*apprendre à vivre*" can
    mean either *learning to live*, that is, *learning oneself to live*, or
    teaching another (or oneself) to live.—TR.]

5   You will have recognized the exordium of *Specters of Marx: The
    State of the Debt, the Work of Mourning, & the New Interna-
    tional*, trans. Peggy Kamuf (New York: Routledge, 1994), xvii;
    the emphasis here is Derrida's.

6 *Specters of Marx*, xix.

7 "Abraham, l'autre, " in Joseph Cohen, Raphael Zaġury-Orly, *Judéités, Questions pour Jacques Derrida* (Paris : Galilée, 2003), 16, 20, 25, 40. [The French here is *acte de naissance*, literally, a "birth certificate."—TR]

8 *Archive Fever*, trans. Eric Prenowitz (Chicago: University of Chicago Press, 1995), 42.

9 *Specters of Marx*, xviii.

10 *Aporias*, trans. Thomas Dutoit (Stanford, CA: Stanford University Press, 1993), 34.

11 "[I]f *tragen* speaks the language of birth, if it must be addressed to a living being present or to come, it can also be addressed to the dead, to the survivor or to their specter, in an experience that consists in bearing the other in the self, just as one bears one's loss or one's mourning—and melancholy," from "Rams : Uninterrupted Dialogue—Between Two Infinities, the Poem," in *Sovereignties in Question: The Poetics of Paul Celan*, edited by Thomas Dutoit and Outi Pasanen (New York: Fordham University Press, 2005), 159.

12 *Aporias*, 55.

13 "Circumfession" in *Jacques Derrida*, by Jacques Derrida and

Geoffrey Bennington, trans. Geoffrey Bennington (Chicago: The University of Chicago Press, 1993), 41.

14 [The word "*alter-mondialist*, " which Derrida returns to later in the interview, is most commonly translated "anti-globalist." But since Derrida is proposing not to abandon all global or world initiatives but to transform them, to help fashion "another," better world, we have opted for "alter-globalist," a term that has gained some currency in certain international movements.—TR.]

15 *Monolinguism of the Other or The Prosthesis of Origin*, trans. Patrick Mensah (Stanford, CA: Stanford University Press, 1996), 47.

16 [1962 is the end of the Algerian "war of independence."—TR.].

17 *The Post Card*, trans. Alan Bass (Chicago: University of Chicago Press, 1987), 184.

18 [In *Monolinguism of the Other* Derrida parses the French word Métropole as "the Capital-City-Mother-Fatherland, the city of the mother tongue" (42).—TR.]

19 *The Other Heading: Reflections on Today's Europe*, trans. Pascale-Anne Brault and Michael Naas (Bloomington, IN: Indiana University Press, 1992), 6–7.

20 [On June 5, 2004, Noël Mamère, mayor of the town of Bègles
in the Gironde region of France, presided over the first same-
sex marriage in France. He was temporarily relieved of his
duties as mayor for performing this illegal ceremony and the
marriage was subsequently annulled by the courts.—TR.]

21 [The word *pacs* is an acronym ("Pacte Civil de Solidarité") for
the provision adopted by French law in 1999 allowing both
heterosexual and same-sex couples to enter into a civil contract
or, translated literally, a "Civil Pact of Solidarity."—TR.]

22 In *On Cosmopolitanism and Forgiveness*, trans. Mark Dooley
and Michael Hughes (London: Routledge, 2001), 1–24.

23 "Autoimmunity: Real and Symbolic Suicides," an interview
with Giovanna Borradori, trans. Pascale-Anne Brault and Michael Naas, in *Philosophy in a Time of Terror*, ed. Giovanna
Borradori (Chicago : University of Chicago Press, 2003), 85–
136, 186–193. The original French version of this interview appears in *Le "concept" du 11 septembre* (Paris : Editions Galilée,
2004).

24 Jacques Derrida, "The University Without Condition," in
Without Alibi, trans. Peggy Kamuf (Stanford, CA: Stanford
University Press, 2002), 50–54.

25 [Robert Faurisson, a well-known Holocaust revisionist
in France, was a professor for many years at the Université
Lyon 2.—TR.]

26 *Chaque fois unique, la fin du monde*, edited by Pascale-Anne Brault and Michael Naas (Paris : Editions Galilée, 2003) [This is the augmented French version of *The Work of Mourning* (Chicago: University of Chicago Press, 2001)]; "Rams" in *Sovereignties in Question: The Poetics of Paul Celan*, 135–163.

27 *The Gift of Death*, trans. David Wills (Chicago: University of Chicago Press, 1995), 12.

28 ["Pas" was first published in 1976 in *Gramma* 3/4, Lire Blanchot 1, and then republished in *Parages* (Paris: Editions Galilée, 1986), 19–116.—TR.]

29 "Signature Event Context," in *Margins of Philosophy*, trans. Alan Bass (Chicago: University of Chicago Press, 1982), 316.

SELECTED BIBLIOGRAPHY

WORKS BY JACQUES DERRIDA PUBLISHED IN ENGLISH

PETER KRAPP

"The Ends of Man." *Philosophy and
Phenomenological Research* 30.1 (1969): 31–57.

"Discussion." *The Structuralist Controversy: The
Languages of Criticism and the Sciences of Man.* Ed.
Richard Macksey & Eugenio Donato. Baltimore:
Johns Hopkins University Press, 1970. 265–272.

"Freud and the Scene of Writing." *Yale
French Studies* 48 (1972): 74–117.

"Letter of Jacques Derrida to Jean-Louis Houdebine
(Excerpt)," *Diacritics* 3.3 (1973): 58–59.

*Speech and Phenomena, and Other Essays on Husserl's Theory
of Signs.* Evanston, IL: Northwestern University Press, 1973.

"Linguistics and Grammatology." *Sub-Stance* 10 (1974): 127–181.

"The White Mythology: Metaphor in the Text of
Philosophy." *New Literary History* 6:1 (1974): 5–74.

"Responses to Questions on the Avant-
Garde." *Digraphe* 6 (Oct 1975): 152–3.

*Spurs: Nietzsche's Styles / Eperons: Les styles de Nietzsche
/ Sporen: die Stile Nietzsches / Sproni: gli stili di Nietzsche.*
Venice: Corbo e Fiori, 1976. (Reprinted Paris: Flammarion
"Champs 41," 1978; and Chicago: Chicago University
Press, 1979, with English and French on facing pages).

"Fors: the Anglish Words of Nicolas Abraham and Maria Torok." *Georgia Review* 31.1 (1976): 64–116.

"From Restricted to General Economy: A Hegelianism without Reserves." *Semiotext(e)* 2.2 (1976): 25–55.

Of Grammatology. Baltimore: Johns Hopkins University Press, 1976.

"The Question of Style." *The New Nietzsche: Contemporary Styles of Interpretation*. Ed. David B. Allison. New York: Delta, 1977, 176–189.

"Signature Event Context." *Glyph* I (1977): 172–97.

"The Purveyor of Truth." *Yale French Studies* 52 (1977): 31–115.

"Becoming Woman." *Semiotext(e)* 3.1 (1978): 128–137.

"Coming into One's Own." *Psychoanalysis and the Question of the Text*. Ed. Geoffrey Hartman. Baltimore: Johns Hopkins University Press, 1978.

Edmund Husserl's Origin of Geometry: An Introduction. New York: Harvester Press, 1978. (Repr.: Lincoln: University of Nebraska Press, 1989.)

"Gérard Titus-Carmel: The Pocket Size Tlingit Coffin." *Gérard Titus-Carmel*. Exhibition March 1-April 10, 1978 at the Centre National d'Art et de

Culture Georges Pompidou, Musée National d"Art
Moderne. Paris: Centre Georges Pompidou, 1978.

"Restitutions of Truth to Size." *Research
in Phenomenology* 8 (1978): 1–44.

"The Retrait of Metaphor." *enclitic* II.2 (1978): 5–34.

"Speech and Writing according to Hegel."
Man and World 11 (1978): 107–130.

"Theater of Cruelty and the Closure of
Representation." *Theater* 9 (1978): 7–19.

Writing and Difference. Chicago: University of Chicago
Press & London: Routledge & Kegan Paul, 1978
(Reissued London: Routledge Classics, 2001)

"Living On: Border Lines." *Deconstruction and
Criticism*. Ed. Geoffrey Hartman. London:
Routledge and Kegan Paul, 1979. 75–176.

"Me—Psychoanalysis: An Introduction to the
Translation of 'The Shell and the Kernel' by
Nicholas Abraham." *Diacritics*, 9:1 (1979): 4–12.

"Parergon." *October* no. 9 (1979): 3–40.

"Scribble (Writing/Power)." *Yale French
Studies* 58 (1979): 116–147.

Spurs: Nietzsche's Styles / Eperons: Les styles de Nietzsche.
Chicago: University of Chicago Press, 1979.

"The SUniversity Pressplement of Copula: Philosophy
before Linguistics." *Textual Strategies: Perspectives in
Post-Structuralist Criticism.* Ed. Josué V. Harari.
London: Methuen 1979, 28–120.

"An Interview with J. Kears and K. Newton." *The
Literary Review* 14.18 April–1 May (1980): 21–22.

"Speculations—On Freud." *Oxford
Literary Review* 3.2 (1980): 80–98.

The Archeology of the Frivolous: Reading Condillac.
Duquesne Philosophical Series, 37. Pittsburgh:
Duquesne University Press 1980. (Reprint:
Lincoln: University of Nebraska Press, 1987).

"The Law of Genre." *Critical Inquiry* 7 (autumn) 1980, 55–81.

Dissemination. Chicago: University of Chicago
Press; London: Athlone Press, 1981.

"Economimesis." *Diacritics* 11 (1981), 3–25.

Positions. London: Athlone, 1981; Chicago:
University of Chicago Press, 1982.

"Title (to be specified)." *Sub-Stance* 31 (1981): 5–22.

"All Ears: Nietzsche's Otobiography." *Yale French Studies* 63 (1982): 245–250.

"Choreographies." *Diacritics* (summer) 1982, 66–76.

"Glas: A selection." *Clio* 11 (1982): 339–360.

"Letter to Colleagues, May 18, 1982." *Sub-Stance* 35 (1982): 2 & 80–81.

"Letter to John P. Leavey, Jr." *Semeia* 23 (1982): 61–62.

"The Linguistic Circle of Geneva." *Critical Inquiry* 8 (1982): 675–691.

Margins of Philosophy. Brighton: Harvester Press; Chicago: University of Chicago Press, 1982.

"Sending: On Representation." *Social Research* 49.2 (1982): 294–326.

"Critical Relation: Peter Szondi's Studies on Célan." *Boundary* 2 11.3 (1983): 155–167.

"Excuse me, but I never said exactly so: Yet Another Derridean Interview." *On The Beach* (Glebe NSW, Australia) 1 (autumn 1983): 43.

"Geschlecht: Sexual Difference, Ontological Difference." *Research in Phenomenology* 13 (1983): 65–83.

"The Principle of Reason: The University in the
Eyes of its Pupils." *Diacritics* 13.3 (1983): 3–20.

"The Time of a Thesis: Punctuations." *Philosophy
in France Today*. Ed. Alan Montefiore. Cambridge:
Cambridge University Press, 1983, 34–50.

"An Idea of Flaubert: Plato's Letter." *Modern
Language Notes* XCIX.4 (1984): 748–68.

"Artists, Philosophers and Institutions." *Rampike*
3:3–4:1 (1984, Institutions, Anti-Institutions), 34–6.

"Deconstruction and the other: Interview with
Richard Kearney." *Dialogues with Contemporary
Thinkers*. Ed. Richard Kearney. Manchester:
Manchester University Press, 1984, 105–126.

"Languages and Institutions of Philosophy."
Semiotic Inquiry 4.2 (1984): 91–154.

"My Chances / Mes Chances: A Rendezvous with
Some Epicurean Stereophonies." *Taking Chances:
Derrida, Psychanalysis, and Literature*. Ed. Joseph
H. Smith and William Kerrigan. Baltimore:
Johns Hopkins University Press, 1984. 1–32.

"No Apocalypse, Not Now (Full Speed Ahead, Seven
Missiles, Seven Missives)." *Diacritics* 14.2 (1984): 20–31.

"Of an Apocalyptic Tone Recently Adopted in Philosophy." *Oxford Literary Review* 6.2 (1984): 3–37.

Signéponge / Signsponge. New York & Guildford: Columbia University Press, 1984. (Parallel French and English text, revised from the earlier versions in the *Oxford Literary Review* 5, 1–2/1982, 96–101 & 102–12.)

"The UnoccUniversity Pressied Chair: Censorship, Mastership and Magistriality." *Semiotic Inquiry* 4.2 (1984): 123–36.

"Two Words for Joyce." *Post-Structuralist Joyce: Essays from the French.* Ed. Daniel Ferrer and Derek Attridge. Cambridge: Cambridge University Press, 1984 148–158.

"Voice II . . ." *Boundary* 2 12.2 (1984): 76–93.

Bernard Tschumi, La Case vide: La Villette, 1985. Eds. Jacques Derrida and Anthony Vidler. London: Architectural Association, 1986. English and French.

"Deconstruction in America: An Interview with Jaques Derrida." *Critical Exchange* 17. Winter (1985): 1–33.

"Des Tours de Babel." *Difference in Translation.* Ed. J. F. Graham. Ithaca and London: Cornell University Press, 1985. 165–207.

"In memoriam: for Paul de Man." *Yale French Studies* 69 (1985): 323–326.

"Interview with Le Nouvel Observateur." *Derrida
and Difference*. Ed. Robert Bernasconi and David
Wood. Warwick: Parousia Press, 1985. 71–82.

"Letter to a Japanese Friend." *Derrida and
Difference*. Eds. Robert Bernasconi and David
Wood. Warwick: Parousia Press, 1985. 1–8.

"Racism's Last Word." *Critical Inquiry* 12.1 (1985): 290–9.

*The Ear of the Other: Otobiography, Transference, Translation:
Texts and Discussions with Jacques Derrida*. Ed. Christie
V. McDonald. New York: Schocken Books, 1985.

"The Age of Hegel." *Demarcating the Disciplines. Philosophy—
Literature—Art*. Ed. Samuel Weber. Minneapolis: University
of Minnesota Press, 1986 (Glyph Textual Studies, vol 1), 3–43.

"But, beyond. . ." *Critical Inquiry* 13. autumn (1986): 155–70.

"Declarations of Independence." *New Political
Science* 15 (summer 1986): 7–15.

"Deconstruction. A Trialogue with Geoffrey
Hartman and Wolfgang Iser." *Mishkenot Sha'ananim
Newsletter* 7. December (1986): Jerusalem.

Glas. Lincoln and London: University of Nebraska Press, 1986.

"Interpreting Signatures (Nietzsche/Heidegger):
Two Questions." *Dialogue and Deconstruction: The*

Gadamer-Derrida Encounter. Ed. Diane P. Michelfelder and
Richard E. Palmer. New York: SUNY Press, 1986. 57–91.

"Interview." *Art Papers* (Atlanta) 10.1 (1986): 31–35.

"Literature and Politics." *New Political
Science* 15 (summer 1986): 5.

Mémoires: For Paul de Man. New York:
Columbia University Press 1986.

"On the University (Interview with Imre Saluzinski)."
Southern Review (Adelaide) 19.1 (March 1986).

"Proverb: He that would pun. . ." *GLASsary*. Ed. John P.
Leavey Jr. Lincoln: University of Nebraska Press, 1986. 17–20.

"A Conversation." *Precis* 6. Columbia University
(1987): Graduate School of Architecture.

For Nelson Mandela. Ed. Jacques Derrida, Mustapha
Tlili. New York: Seaver Books, 1987.

"Geschlecht 2: Heidegger's Hand." *Deconstruction
and Philosophy*. Ed. John Sallis. Chicago:
University of Chicago Press, 1987.

"Interview with Imre Saluzinski." *Criticism in Society*.
Ed. Imre Saluzinski. London: Methuen, 1987.

"Interview with Jeff Bernard." *Semiotica Austriaca*. Wien, 1987.

The Archeology of the Frivolous: Reading Condillac.
Lincoln: University of Nebraska Press, 1987.

The Post Card: From Socrates to Freud and Beyond. Chicago
& London: University of Chicago Press, 1987.

The Truth in Painting. Chicago: University
of Chicago Press, 1987.

"Reply," *Men in Feminism.* Eds. Alice Jardine
and Paul Smith. London: Methuen, 1987.

"Some Questions and Responses." *The Linguistics of
Writing.* Eds. Attridge, Fabb, Durant and McCabe.
Manchester: Manchester University Press, 1987. 252–264.

"A Number of Yes (Nombre de oui)." *Qui
Parle* 2.2 (1988): 120–133.

"Afterword: Toward an Ethic of Discussion."
Limited Inc. Ed. Gerald Graff. Evanston, Il.:
Northwestern University Press, 1988. 111–154.

"Point of Folly." *Arch Plus* 95, November-
December 1988, 54–63.

Choral Work. Jacques Derrida and Peter
Eisenman. London: AA Publications, 1988.

"The Deaths of Roland Barthes." *Continental Philosophy I: Philosophy and Non-Philosophy since Merleau-Ponty*. Ed. Hugh Silverman. London: Routledge 1988, 259–296.

"The Derridean View." *BM 4* (Sept. 1988): City University of New York.

"Fifty-Two Aphorisms for a Foreword." *Deconstruction: Omnibus*. Tate Gallery/Academy Forum. London: 1988.

Interview with Jean-Luc Nancy, *Topoi* 7 (1988), 113–121.

"Like the Sound of the Sea Deep Within a Shell: Paul de Man's War." *Critical Inquiry* 14, spring (1988): 590–652. (Reprinted in *Responses: On Paul de Man's Wartime Journalism*. Eds. W. Hamacher, N. Hertz, T. Keenan. Lincoln: University of Nebraska Press, 127–164.)

Limited Inc. Evanston: Northwestern University Press, 1988. (Repr. from *Glyph* #1-#2, 1977: 162–254. Baltimore: Johns Hopkins University Press, 1977.)

"The New Modernism: Deconstructionist Tendencies in Art." *Art & Design* 8 (1988), 3–4.

"On Reading Heidegger: An Outline of Remarks to the Essex Colloquium." *Research in Phenomenology* 17 (1988): 171–188.

"The Politics of Friendship." *Journal of Philosophy* 75.11 (1988): 632–45.

"Telepathy." *Oxford Literary Review*
10. Anniversary Issue (1988): 3–41.

"Why Peter Eisenman Writes Such Good Books."
Threshold: Journal of the School of Architecture. University
of Illinois at Chicago (Spring 1988), 4:99–105.

"Biodegradables: Seven Diary Fragments."
Critical Inquiry 15.4 (1989): 812–873.

"Desistance." *Typography: Mimesis, Philosophy,
Politics*. Ed. Philippe Lacoue-Labarthe. Cambridge:
Harvard University Press, 1989. 1–42.

"The Ghost Dance: An Interview with Jacques
Derrida." *Public* 2/1989, 60–74.

"How to Avoid Speaking: Denials." *Derrida
and Negative Theology*. Ed. Harold Coward and
Toby Foshay. Albany: SUNY Press, 1989.

"How to Concede, with Reasons?" *Diacritics* 19.3–4 (1989): 4–9.

"In conversation with Christopher Norris."
Architectural Design 58.1–2 (1989): 6–11.

"Not Everybody Loves a Parade (interview with Scott
L. Malcomson)." *Village Voice* July 25th 1989: 29–32.

"Of Spirit." *Critical Inquiry* 15 (1989): 457–474.

Of Spirit: Heidegger and the Question. Chicago: Chicago University Press, 1989.

"On Colleges and Philosophy." *Postmodernism: ICA Documents*.Ed. Lisa Appignanesi. New York: Columbia University Press, 1989. 66–71.

"Right of Inspection." *Art & Text* 32 (1989): 19–97.

"Some Statements and Truisms about Neologisms, Newisms, Postisms, Parasitisms, and other small Seismisms." *The States of Theory*. Ed. D. Carroll. New York: Columbia University Press, 1989. 63–94.

"A Discussion with Jacques Derrida." *Writing Instructor*, USC 9.1–2 (1990): 7–18.

"A letter to Peter Eisenman." *Assemblage: A Critical Journal of Architecture and Design* 12 (August 1990).

"Force of Law: The Mystical Foundation of Authority." *Cardozo Law Review: Deconstruction and the Possibility of Justice*. 11:5–6 (1990): 920–1045.

"Interview." *French Philosophers in Conversation*. Ed. Raoul Mortley. London: Routledge, 1990. 93–108

"Let us not Forget—Psychoanalysis." *Oxford Literary Review* 12 (1990): 3–7.

"On Rhetoric and Composition (Conversation
with Gary Olson)." *Journal of Advanced
Composition*, USF 10.1 (1990): 1–21.

"Sendoffs." *Yale French Studies* 77 (1990): 7–43.

"Subverting the Signature: A Theory of the Parasite."
Blast Unlimited (Boston) 2 (1990): 16–21.

"The Philosopher sees (or doesn't see)." *The Art Newspaper*
vol. 1 no. 1, Oct. 1990.

"Women in the Beehive." *Discourses: Conversations in
Postmodern Art and Culture*. Ed. R. Ferguson. London: MIT
Press, 1990. 115–128 (Repr. from *Men in Feminism*, eds. Alice
Jardine and Paul Smith, London: Routledge, 1987. 115–128)

"At This Very Moment in This Work Here I Am." *Re-Reading
Levinas*. Ed. Robert Bernasconi and Simon Critchley.
Bloomington: Indiana University Press, 1991. 11–48.

Between the Blinds. Ed. Peggy Kamuf. New
York: Columbia University Press, 1991.

Cinders. Lincoln: University of Nebraska Press, 1991.

"Eating Well, or the Calculation of the Subject."
Who Comes After the Subject? Eds. Connor, Nancy,
Cadava. London: Routledge, 1991. 96–119.

"Fragment of a letter." *Textual Practice* no. 5, 1991.

"Interpretations at War: Kant, the Jew, the German." *New Literary History* 22 (1991): 39–95.

"Interventions." *Zeitgeist in Babel: The Postmodernist Controversy.* Ed. Ingeborg Hoesterey. Bloomington: Indiana University Press, 1991.

"Memories of a Blind Man." *Art International* 14 spring/summer (1991): 82–7.

"Sight Unseen." *Art in America* 79 (April 1991): 47–53.

"Summary of Impromptu Remarks, 58 minutes, 41 seconds." *Anyone.* Ed. Cynthia C. Davidson. New York: Rizzoli, 1991.

"This is not an oral footnote." *Annotation and its Texts.* Ed. Stephen A Barney. Oxford: Oxford University Press, 1991.

Acts of Literature. Ed. Derek Attridge. London: Routledge, 1992.

"Afterw.rds" *Afterwords.* Ed. Nicholas Royle. Tampere: Outside Books, 1992. 197–203.

"Canons and Metonymies." *Logomachia.* Ed. Richard Rand. Lincoln: University of Nebraska Press, 1992.

"Given Time: The Time of the King." *Critical Inquiry* 18/2 (Winter 1992): 161–187.

"Invitation to a Discussion." *Columbia Documents
of Architecture and Theory*, vol 1: D (1992), 7–27.

"Mochlos, or The Conflict of the Faculties."
Logomachia. Ed. Richard Rand. Lincoln:
University of Nebraska Press, 1992. 1–34.

"Onto-Theology of National-Humanism. (Prolegomena to
a Hypothesis)." *Oxford Literary Review* 14.1–2 (1992): 3–24.

"Passions: An Oblique Offering." *Derrida: A Critical
Reader*. Ed. David Wood. Oxford: Blackwell, 1992. 5–35.

"Post-Scriptum: Aporias, Ways and Voices." *Derrida
and Negative Theology*. Ed. Harold Coward and
Toby Foshay. Albany: SUNY Press, 1992.

"Schibboleth." *Word Traces*. Ed. Aris Fioretis.
Baltimore: Johns Hopkins University Press, 1992.

The Other Heading: Reflections on Today's Europe.
Bloomington: Indiana University Press, 1992.

"This Strange Institution Called Literature." *Acts of
Literature*. Ed. Derek Attridge. London: Routledge, 1992.

"Ulysses Gramophone: Hear Say Yes in
Joyce." *Acts of Literature*. Ed. Derek Attridge.
London: Routledge, 1992. 253ff.

Aporias: dying—awaiting (one another at) the "limits of truth." Stanford: Stanford University Press, 1993.

"Back from Moscow, in the USSR." *Jacques Derrida in Moscow.* Ed. Mikhail Ryklin. Moscow: Ad Marginem, 1993. 13–81.

"Back from Moscow, in the USSR." *Politics, Theory, and Contemporary Culture.* Ed. Mark Poster. Columbia University Press, 1993. 197–235

"Circonfession." *Jacques Derrida.* Chicago: University of Chicago Press, 1993.

Given Time: The Time of the King. Vol. I: Counterfeit Money. Chicago: University of Chicago Press, 1993.

"Heidegger's Ears. Geschlecht IV: Philopolemology." *Reading Heidegger. Commemorations.* Ed. John Sallis, Bloomington and Indianapolis: 1993. 163–218.

Jacques Derrida. Jacques Derrida and Geoffrey Bennington. Chicago: University of Chicago Press 1993.

"Le toucher: Touch/to touch him." *Paragraph* 16/2 (July 1993): 124–157.

Memoirs of the blind: the self-portrait and other ruins. Chicago: University of Chicago Press, 1993.

"Talking about Writing" (with Peter Eisenman). *Anyone* (1993), 18–21.

"The Rhetoric of Drugs. An Interview."
Differences vol. 5, no. 1 (1993): 1–25.

"Foreword." *The Hélène Cixous Reader*. Ed. Susan
Sellers. London: Routledge, 1994. 200.

"Nietzsche and the Machine." *Journal of
Nietzsche Studies* 7 (1994): 7–66.

*Specters of Marx: The State of the Debt, the Work of Mourning,
& the New International*. London: Routledge, 1994.

"The Deconstruction of Actuality." *Radical
Philosophy* no 68 (1994), 28–41.

"The Time is Out of Joint." *Deconstruction is/in America*.
Ed. A. Haverkamp. New York: NYU, 1994. 14–38.

"To Do Justice To Freud." *Foucault and His
Interlocutors*. Ed Arnold I. Davidson. Chicago:
University of Chicago Press, 1997. 57–96.

"Applied Derrida." (Interview). *Writing in Reserve:
Deconstruction on the Net*, 1995ff. Ed. Peter Krapp
(*www.hydra.umn.edu/derrida/*), repr. "As if I were Dead: An
Interview with Jacques Derrida," *Applying: to Derrida*. Ed.
John Brannigan et al., London: Macmillan 1997. 212–226.

"Archive Fever. A Freudian Impression."
Diacritics 25/2 (Summer) 1995, 9–63.

The Gift of Death. Chicago: University of Chicago Press, 1995.

On the Name. Stanford: Stanford University Press, 1995.

Points: Interviews 1974–1994. Ed. Elisabeth Weber.
Stanford: Stanford University Press, 1995.

"Tense." *The Path of Archaic Thinking.* Ed.
Kenneth Maly, Albany: SUNY 1995.

"Villanova Conversations." *Writing in Reserve:
Deconstruction on the Net*, 1995ff. Ed. Peter Krapp.
(*www.hydra.umn.edu/derrida/*). Repr. as "The Villanova
Roundtable: A Conversation with Jacques Derrida,"
Deconstruction in a Nutshell. Ed. John D. Caputo.
New York: Fordham University Press 1997, 4–28.

"Adieu." *Philosophy Today* 40 (3) 1996, 33–340.

Archive Fever: A Freudian Impression. Chicago:
University of Chicago Press, 1996.

"A demi-mot." *America's Modernisms: Revaluing
the Canon. Essays in Honor of Joseph N. Riddel.*
Eds. Kathryne V. Lindberg and Joseph Kronick.
Louisiana State University Press, 1996.

"By force of mourning." *Critical Inquiry* 22, n. 2 (winter 1996).

"Der Philosoph und die Architekten / The Philosopher
and the Architects." *Paper Art 6: Dekonstruktivistische*

Tendenzen / Deconstructivist Tendencies. Ed. Dorothea
Eimert. Ostfildern: Cantz Verlag 1996, 84–87.

*Edmund Husserl's Origin of Geometry: An
Introduction.* Moscow: Ad Marginem, 1996.

"Remarks on deconstruction and pragmatism."
Deconstruction and Pragmatism. Ed. Chantal
Mouffe. New York, Routledge, 1996.

*Chora L works: Jacques Derrida and Peter
Eisenman.* Eds. Jeffrey Kipnis and Thomas
Leeser. New York : Monacelli Press, 1997.

"...et grenades..." *Violence, Identity and Self-
Determination,.*Eds. Hent de Vries and Samuel
Weber. Stanford: Stanford University Press: 1997.

"History of the Lie: Prolegomena." *Graduate Faculty
Philosophical Journal* 19/20 (2/1) 1997, 129–161.

Politics of Friendship. London: Verso Books, 1997.

"A Silkworm of One's Own." *Oxford
Literary Review* 18 (1997), 3–65.

*Monolingualism of the other, or, The prosthesis of
origin.* Stanford: Stanford University Press, 1998.

Resistances: of Psychoanalysis. Stanford:
Stanford University Press, 1998.

Right of Inspection. New York : Monacelli Press, 1998.

The Derrida Reader: Writing Performances. Ed. Julian Wolfreys. Edinburgh: Edinburgh University Press, 1998.

Religion. Ed. Jacques Derrida and Gianni Vattimo. Stanford: Stanford University Press, 1998.

The secret art of Antonin Artaud (with Paule Thévenin). Cambridge: MIT Press, 1998.

Adieu to Emmanuel Levinas. Stanford: Stanford University Press, 1999.

"Marx and Sons," *Ghostly Demarcations.* Ed. Michael Sprinker. London: Verso 1999.

Raising the tone of philosophy: late essays by Immanuel Kant, Transformative critique by Jacques Derrida. Ed. Peter Fenves. Baltimore: Johns Hopkins University Press, 1999.

"Et cetera. . ." *Deconstructions.* Ed. Nicholas Royle. London: Palgrave, 2000. 282–305.

Of hospitality / Anne Dufourmantelle invites Jacques Derrida to respond. Stanford: Stanford University Press, 2000

"Word Processing." *Oxford Literary Review* 21 (2000), 3–17.

Demeure: Fiction and Testimony. Stanford: Stanford University Press, 2000.

Acts of Religion. London: Routledge 2001.

A Taste for the Secret (with Maurizio Ferrari). London: Polity Press, 2001.

Futures: of Jacques Derrida. Ed. Richard Rand. Stanford: Stanford University Press 2001.

"Circumfession periphrases." *Body of Prayer.* New York: Cooper Union, 2001.

Deconstruction Engaged: The Sydney Seminars. Sydney: Power Institute, 2001.

On Cosmopolitanism and Forgiveness. London: Routledge 2001.

"To forgive. The unforgivable and the imprescriptible." *Questioning God.* Ed. J. Caputo et al. Bloomington: Indiana University Press, 2001. 21–51.

The Work of Mourning. Chicago: University of Chicago Press, 2001.

Veils (with Hélène Cixous). Stanford: Stanford University Press, 2001.

"What Is a 'Relevant' Translation?" *Critical Inquiry* 27 (2001): 174–200.

Echographies of Television: Filmed Interviews. London: Polity Press, 2002.

Ethics, Institutions, and the Right to Philosophy. Ed. Peter
Pericles Trifonas. Lanham, Md.: Rowman & Littlefield, 2002.

*Negotiations: Interventions and Interviews, 1971–
2001.* Ed. Elizabeth G. Rottenberg. Stanford:
Stanford University Press, 2002.

"The three ages of Jacques Derrida." Interview with
Kristine McKenna. *LA Weekly* November 8–14 2002.

*Who's Afraid of Philosophy?: Right to Philosophy
I.* Stanford: Stanford University Press 2002.

Without Alibi. Stanford: Stanford University Press, 2002.

"The becoming possible of the impossible: an
interview." *Passion for the Impossible: John D.
Caputo in Focus.* Albany: SUNY Press, 2003.

"Call it a day for democracy." *Kettering Review* 21:1 (fall 2003).

The Problem of Genesis in Husserl's Philosophy. Translated by
Marian Hobson. Chicago: University of Chicago Press 2003.

*Philosophy in a Time of Terror: Dialogues With Jürgen
Habermas and Jacques Derrida.* Ed. Giovanna Borradori.
Chicago: University of Chicago Press, 2003.

The Work of Mourning. Chicago: University
of Chicago Press, 2003.

Counterpath: Traveling With Jacques Derrida, interviews with
Catherine Malabou. Stanford: Stanford University Press, 2004.

Eyes of the University: Right to Philosophy vol 2.
Stanford: Stanford University Press, 2004.

*For What Tomorrow: A Dialogue with Elisabeth
Roudinesco.* Stanford: Stanford University Press, 2004.

"Out of Joint: Obituary for Heiner Müller," in Peter Krapp,
Déja Vu: Aberrations of Cultural Memory. Minneapolis:
University of Minnesota Press, 2004. 206–207.

Questioning Judaism: Interviews by Elisabeth Weber.
Stanford: Stanford University Press, 2004.

*Sovereignties in Question: The Poetics of Paul
Celan.* Eds. Thomas Dutoit and Outi Pasanen.
New York: Fordham University Press, 2005.

Paper Machine. Stanford: Stanford University Press, 2005.

Rogues: Two Essays on Reason. Stanford:
Stanford University Press, 2005.

"How to name." *Recumbents: Poems by Michel
Deguy.* Ed. Wilson Baldridge. Middletown,
Conn.: Wesleyan University Press, 2005.

On touching, Jean-Luc Nancy. Stanford:
Stanford University Press, 2005.

The Derrida-Habermas Reader. Ed. Lasse Thomassen. Chicago: University of Chicago Press, 2006.

Geneses, Genealogies, Genres, and Genius: The Secrets of the Archive. New York: Columbia University Press, 2006.

H.C. for life, that is to say—. Stanford: Stanford University Press, 2006.

OTHER BIBLIOGRAPHIES ON DERRIDA AND DECONSTRUCTION

Attridge, Derek. "A Selected Bibliography of Jacques Derrida's Writing, with particular reference to the question of literature." *Acts of Literature*. Ed. Derek Attridge. London: Routledge, 1992, 435–442.

Barney, Richard. "Deconstructive Criticism: A Selected Bibliography." *SCE Reports* (Society for Critical Exchange) 8/1980.

Bennington, Geoffrey. "Bibliographie." *Jacques Derrida* by G. Bennington and J. Derrida, 355–419.

Berns, Egide: "Jacques Derrida." *Kritisch Denkerslexicon*, 3, 1987.

Culler, J.: *On Deconstruction: Theory and Criticism after Structuralism*. Ithaca: Cornell University Press, 1982.

Daniel, M.: "A bibliography of Derrida and phenomenology."
W. R. McKenna und J. C. Evans. *Derrida and
Phenomenology*. Boston, Kluwer Academic Publishers, 1995.

Ferraris, Maurizio. *Postille a Derrida*.
Torino: Rosenberg & Sellier, 1990

Fried, Lewis L.B. und William R. Schultz. *Jacques
Derrida: An Annotated Primary and Secondary
Bibliography*. New York: Garland, 1992.

Hulbert, J. *Jacques Derrida: An annotated
Bibliography*. New York, Garland, 1984.

Krapp, Peter. "Derrida Online." 1994–2007:
www.hydra.umn.edu/derrida/

Leavey, John and Allison, David. "A Derrida Bibliography."
Research in Phenomenology 8 (1978), 145–160.

Leventure, Albert. "A Jacques Derrida Bibliography
1962–1990." *Textual Practice* 5.1 (Spring) 1991.

Leventure, Albert, and Keenan, Thomas. "A Bibliography of
the Works of Jacques Derrida." *Derrida: A Critical Reader*.
Ed. David Wood. Oxford: Blackwell, 1992, 247–289.

Lisse, Michel. *Jacques Derrida*. Bruxelles: Hatier, 1986.

Nordquist, Joan. *Jacques Derrida: A Bibliography*.
New York: Reference and Research Services, 1986.

Nordquist, Joan. *Jacques Derrida II: A Bibliography*.
New York: Reference and Research Services, 1995.

Norris, Christopher. *Deconstruction: Theory
and Practice*. London: Methuen, 1982.

Norris, Christopher. *Derrida*. Cambridge:
Harvard University Press, 1988.

Orr, L. "Bibliography." *Sub-Stance* 22 (1979).

Peretti, C. "Jacques Derrida: una bibliografía (de 1962 a
1988)". *Anthropos. Revista de Documentación Científica de la
Cultura (Barcelona)* "SUniversity Presslementos" 13 (l989).

Sertoli, G. "Jacques Derrida: una bibliografia,"
Nuova Corrente 28 (1981) 84.

Vidarte, Paco. "Traductions en Espagnol des Textes de Derrida."
Derrida Online, www.hydra.umn.edu/derrida/esp.html

Weber, Elisabeth. "Bibliography of Other Interviews with
Jacques Derrida." *Points: Interviews 1974–1994*. Ed. E.
Weber. Stanford: Stanford University Press, 1995, 495–499.

Yeghiayan, Eddie. "Derrida." (sun3.lib.uci.edu/indiv/
scctr/hri/postmodern/) Special Collections, Main
Library, University of California, Irvine, CA 92697.

THE LAST INTERVIEW SERIES

KURT VONNEGUT: THE LAST INTERVIEW

"I think it can be tremendously refreshing if a creator of literature has something on his mind other than the history of literature so far. Literature should not disappear up its own asshole, so to speak."

$15.95 / $17.95 CAN
978-1-61219-090-7
ebook: 978-1-61219-091-4

LEARNING TO LIVE FINALLY: THE LAST INTERVIEW
JACQUES DERRIDA

"I am at war with myself, it's true, you couldn't possibly know to what extent . . . I say contradictory things that are, we might say, in real tension; they are what construct me, make me live, and will make me die."

translated by PASCAL-ANNE BRAULT and MICHAEL NAAS

$15.95 / $17.95 CAN
978-1-61219-094-5
ebook: 978-1-61219-032-7

ROBERTO BOLAÑO: THE LAST INTERVIEW

"Posthumous: It sounds like the name of a Roman gladiator, an unconquered gladiator. At least that's what poor Posthumous would like to believe. It gives him courage."

translated by SYBIL PEREZ and others

$15.95 / $17.95 CAN
978-1-61219-095-2
ebook: 978-1-61219-033-4